oMa tElls 'HiS'toRiEs!

Oma tells 'His'tories

A Devotional book for parents to share with their children

Ages 2-8

Oma Tells Histories
by Dina van Beek

Signalman Publishing 2012
www.signalmanpublishing.com
email: info@signalmanpublishing.com
Kissimmee, Florida

Front cover artwork and illustrations by Daniel van Magill.

ISBN: 978-1-935991-45-8 (paperback)
       978-1-935991-46-5 (ebook)

Signalman
Publishing

Table of Contents

Acknowledgements

This little book is dedicated to my great grandchildren:
Charlotte, Annie, Bethany, Emily, Jacob, Phoebe, Ryan and those yet to be born.

My sincere thanks to Kath Fauchon, her advice and setting me off on this path has been great.
Thanks, Kath.

All Things Bright and Beautiful

Come along with me and we'll have a look at your backyard. What do you see? Are there any flowers in your garden? Have a look. In my garden there are nice red roses, white flowers, pink ones and lovely trees, where the birds call each other. I look up at the sky and see a beautiful blue sky, the sun, and sometimes clouds. At night the moon may be there and also many stars. Too many to count. When we drive to the country, we see sheep, cattle, kangaroos, emus, and lots of other animals, don't we? What do we see at the beach? Lots of shells, sand, and fish swimming in the water. There is so much to see. And God made them all.

God made Adam and Eve and told them to look after all he had made. He told them to take charge of it, but said if they ate a certain fruit they would be in trouble and die. Did they listen and obey God? No they did not and they got into trouble.

We are sometimes like that too. We might think we know better than Mum or Dad and do what we want to do, no matter what. What happens then? We also get into trouble, don't we?

And what will happen if we keep on being naughty and doing the wrong things?

I will tell you what happens in my next story.

For now, look in your garden, count all the beautiful things you see, but don't pick any of them without asking first.

Prayer: Thank you, Lord, for giving us such a beautiful world to live in.

Noah's Ark

God made all things in this world and he made Adam and Eve. I told you in my previous story; Adam and Eve did not obey God and got into trouble. They had to leave their beautiful garden and they went their own way, not God's way. The world was not a nice place anymore. There were lots of fights and people were killing each other. God felt sorry that it had gone that way. There was one man and his family, however, who loved God and wanted to obey him. His name was Noah. God told Noah to build an ark (or big boat) and told him exactly how big it was to be. It had to be very big because he wanted lots of animals in the boat.

It was a huge job and it took Noah a very long time to build. I am sure that many people would have asked him why he was building such a big boat. He told them God wanted him to do it and that there would be a very big flood one day and everything would be under water. The people did not believe him and even laughed at him and made jokes. Rain – they did not even know what rain was. Noah obeyed God and built the ark.

When the ark was finished, Noah and his family went into the ark with two of every kind of animal. Then the rain came down. It rained for a very long time. Day after day, week after week, and month after month it rained. No one was able to go and play outside. It must have been a very hard time for all the animals, but for Noah and his family as well, don't you think?

How happy they were when at last it stopped raining and they could leave the ark. Noah and his family thanked God for saving them. They had a hard time in the ark, and God promised that he would never do something like that again. He gave us a beautiful rainbow to remind us of this promise he made.

So every time you see a rainbow, you know that God promised never to destroy all the earth with a flood again.

A Baby Born

I love babies. Don't you? Do you have a baby brother or sister? Perhaps your Mum lets you hold the baby on your lap for a while. They are so beautiful. Look at their little fingers and toes. They are so cute. When they smile and giggle at you, then you feel so happy and want to cuddle them. Sometimes though, they have a dirty nappy and you hand them quickly back to Mum don't you? Why do mums have the yucky jobs? Mums don't mind because they love their children so very much.

This story is about a lady named Hannah. She had no children and she wanted a baby SO much. She saw mums with their babies in the park and wished and wished that she had a little one to look after. She would not mind cleaning their dirty nappies at all.

Once a year, Hannah and her husband would go to the big city where special services were held in the Temple (church). It was a long way from home. There were no cars, buses or trains in those days and they had to walk.

One year when Hannah and her husband went to the big city Temple, she was especially sad. She was on her own in the Temple and was crying because she was so sad. Hannah was asking the Lord to give her a baby. Her lips were moving but no one could hear what she was saying. She was praying silently.

The priest Eli sat in the front so he could see everybody. He thought that she had been drinking wine. He was very angry that she dared to come to the Temple drunk. He went straight up to her and planned to tell her off. Hannah told him that she had not been drinking but was very sad and was praying to God about it.

The priest knew he had made a big mistake and blessed her before she left the Temple.

One year passed and it was time to go to the Temple again. This time she was so happy because she had a little son. She named him Samuel. God had granted Hannah her heart's desire for a baby. She loved her little boy very much. I wonder how much she spoilt him?

Do you think that Hannah thanked God for answering her prayers?

Let us see what happened next to Hannah and her son Samuel.

Hannah had one big problem. You remember she prayed to God with tears in her eyes? Well she promised God if He would give her a child, she would hand him back to God so he could become a priest and serve God all the days of his life.

That was a very big promise.

The Temple where the priest lived was a long way from home and Samuel would have to live there. Hannah would see her boy only once a year. That must have been a very hard thing to do for both of them, don't you think? Can you remember your first day at school? Was it hard for you to leave your Mum for the first time? I bet it was difficult for Mum as well. She missed you just like you missed her. But she promised to be there at the gate in the afternoon. Can you remember how happy your Mum was to see you and how happy you were to see her? You could tell her all about what happened during the day and all about your new teacher.

If Hannah kept her promise to God, she would not see Samuel every day. She would see her boy only once a year. But she had made a promise. What was she going to do? Keep her promise or say, "God will understand that I cannot do this."

"It was very difficult but she kept her promise and sent him to that special school to learn all about God. This was so difficult for both of them, but you know what? God blessed Hannah and Samuel for keeping that promise. Samuel became a prophet and leader of the people. As an important leader he even talked with Kings.

Sometimes we have to make very difficult decisions but God will bless us if we keep our promises.

Questions:
How would you feel if you had to leave your Mum and Dad and live in a far away place? Do you think God understood how Samuel and his Mum felt?

Prayer: Dear Lord, I thank you for my Mum and Dad and I ask you to bless them. Amen.

A Young Boy Became King

A young boy named David had seven brothers. How would you feel if you had seven big brothers? David was the youngest and I wonder if he would have been spoilt by his big brothers... or bullied? Let us see what we can find out about David.

His job was to look after his father's sheep. His brothers had more important jobs to do. David loved to play the harp and he was so good at it that later on he used to play for the king.

One day the Prophet Samuel (remember young Samuel from the last story – he was now grown up) arrived in the town where David lived. Everybody was excited about it. Samuel asked David's father Jesse to come with all his sons to a great feast. All the people were looking forward to it. Samuel had a special reason to ask for all of Jesse's family to be there. God told him to anoint one of Jesse's sons to be King. He did not know which of the sons it would be, but the Lord would tell him when he saw him.

All of Jesse's sons (except David) gathered together and Samuel met the first son and thought, surely this must be the one. He is so good looking, he is strong and he speaks nicely.

But...

God said, "No, he is not the one."

Samuel met all the sons one by one and God said, "No, this is not the one."

How puzzled Samuel must have been. Was God playing a trick on him? At last Samuel asked Jesse, "Are all your sons here?"

"No," Jesse said, "the youngest son is not here. He is watching the sheep."

I wonder why the youngest son was not there? Samuel had asked Jesse for all his sons to be there. Why not David? Was it because David was not important enough? Or perhaps it was because he was only a boy and too young to be with all the grown ups? Did he really have to look after the sheep? Somehow I don't think so because Samuel said, "We will not start until he is here." So Jesse quickly sent for him.

Samuel took one look at David and the Lord told him that he was the one chosen to be the King of Israel.

What a surprise it must have been for Samuel when God told him that David was the one. A young boy for a king? The Lord told Samuel that people look at the outside appearance, but God looks at the heart. God knew David would make a good king.

You and I might not be very beautiful or handsome on the outside (perhaps we are but we don't think so ourselves) but we can be beautiful on the inside, which is far more important. The Lord chooses people to do important things based on what he sees in their heart.

We all want to be beautiful on the outside, but do you want to be beautiful on the inside? Let us ask God to make us beautiful on the inside.

Prayer:
Dear Lord, will you help me to become good and kind? I want to be a person you can use. Just like you chose David for an important job, I want you to use me. In Jesus name. Amen.

Jonah Playing Hide and Seek

Have you ever played hide and seek with your friends? It is lots of fun isn't it.

Remember the game where everyone has to hide and one person has to look for him or her?

That one person stands in a corner with their eyes closed and counts... "1, 2, 3, 4, 5, 6, 7, 8, 9, 10... ready or not, here I come!" He or she will look for you and tap you on the shoulder when you are found.

God told Jonah to go to a very big city named Nineveh. A lot of bad people lived in that city. God wanted Jonah to go to them and tell them that if they did not change, the city would be destroyed in forty days.

Jonah hated that city and did not want to go there. He thought, "If I go on a boat trip in the opposite direction to Nineveh, surely God will not find me." He was hiding from God.

In the boat at sea, there was a very big storm. It scared everybody on the boat. The storm was so bad that people on the boat thought that there was something very wrong. They asked each other, "What has happened?" Jonah realised that he was the cause of the storm. He told the men they will have to throw him overboard. If they did, everything would be fine again. It must have been very hard for him to say that. The men did not like to do it but they were all in danger and it was better that one person should die than for all of them to be drowned.

So they tossed him overboard and sure enough, the sea became calm again. Everybody was saved. But what happened to poor Jonah? He was swallowed by a very big fish... as big as a whale. He went straight into the fish's belly. In the belly of the fish, he cried out to God and God heard his cries and brought him back to the beach.

Jonah learned a very big lesson. You cannot hide from God. He obeyed God and went to Nineveh. All the people in that city believed what God told Jonah to tell them. They said they were sorry for being bad and God forgave them.

Questions: Do you think that you can hide from God? If you do something wrong and you are sorry, will God forgive you? Did he forgive Nineveh?

Naaman Healed of Leprosy

A very important man named Naaman was the commander of a great army. He was a good man but he got sick with a horrible skin disease that kept him awake at night.

One day, his soldiers took a very young slave girl from Israel to him. The poor girl was taken away from her mum and dad and was now living in a strange country. Naaman's wife took her as a helper in the home and was kind to this young girl.

When the girl heard about Naaman's skin disease, she wanted to help him and told him that in her country of Samaria, there lived a prophet who would be able to help. She did not know what part of Samaria. She did not even know his name.

When Naaman heard about this, he believed the girl and he asked his Boss (the King) if he could go and try to find him. The King even gave him a very nice letter and told him that he wanted Naaman to be cured of his disease. Naaman found out where the prophet lived and that his name was Elisha. Naaman went straight to his house. Elisha did not even go out to meet this important man but sent a message to him telling him to go and wash himself seven times in the Jordan River. Naaman did not like to go to that dirty river but he did it because his friends encouraged him to do it. Naaman was healed. He was so happy.

If it were not for that little slave girl, he would not have been healed, would he?

People sometimes say that children should be seen and not heard. In this story, however, don't you think that Naaman was wise to listen to this little girl? If we know something that can help others, we should speak up. God can use little people and big people. We are all very important to him.

Prayer: I know that you, God, love me and I want others to know that you love them too. Help me to tell others.

Mary and Joseph

Mary and Joseph had to leave Nazareth and walk all the way to Bethlehem. Why, you may ask? Well, the leader of the country wanted to know how many people were living in the country and each one had to go to the place where they were born. There were no cars or bikes so they had to walk (or ride on a donkey) all the way and it was a very long walk for Joseph and Mary. Mary was expecting a baby as well. I'm sure if your mum and dad had to go that far they would hop in the car and be there in no time. They would probably also telephone a motel to make sure they had a place to stay.

Mary and Joseph walked and walked and walked. Sometimes Mary would sit on a donkey for some of the way but she was getting tired and wished they were there. It was getting dark and cold. At last they saw some houses. "Great," Mary thought, "now we are nearly there." How happy she must have been.

At the first motel they saw, they stopped and rang the bell. The owner came out and when Joseph asked for a room, the owner said, "I am so sorry, I am fully booked. I have no rooms left."

What was going to happen? Mary was so tired and worried. I'll bet she had a little cry. Then Joseph tried another motel. The owner came out and said he did not have any room. Joseph must have felt so sorry for Mary. She must have been so sad and disappointed.

Then the man said, "I have a stable (like a barn or shed). It is not very nice but we can clean it up. At least you will have shelter for the night and we can make it reasonably comfortable for you."

Mary and Joseph were very happy to take it – at least it was better than having to sleep outdoors.

Sometimes we have hard times and we feel like crying but "underneath are the everlasting arms" of the Lord and he will help us to carry on. You can trust him. Mary and Joseph did settle in the stable and Jesus was born there. Important visitors came to visit them there.

The First Christmas

Away in a manger,
No crib for a bed,
The little Lord Jesus
Lay down his sweet head.

We sing that carol at Christmas time, don't we?

I am wondering why Jesus was born in a manger. Why wasn't he born in a palace or a castle? After all, he is God's Son. He is worthy to be born in a palace or a castle, or at least a beautiful big home.

It does not sound fair to me that he was born in a stable with lots of animals. It must have been pretty smelly in that place. When we were born, we had a lovely soft bed. We didn't have to sleep in a manger, an animal's feeding trough. It must have been very hard and uncomfortable for little Lord Jesus.

But if he had been born in a palace, would he understand what it is like to live like us? A queen or prince may visit the poor people and try to understand how it would feel to live in a shed or even sleep in a park but they have never done it.

Jesus became just like one of us so that he could understand us perfectly. He loves us so much, he willingly came to live among us and be one of us.

I am so glad Jesus loves us, aren't you?

I Am The Good Shepherd

Jesus said, "I am the Good Shepherd."

Jesus told a story about ten sheep. The shepherd looked after those ten sheep. He made sure they had enough to eat and he saved them from danger such as wolves. In the cold weather, he protected them.

Those ten sheep were well cared for but one sheep got lost. How did he get lost, I wonder? Well perhaps he did not like to listen to the shepherd and thought he could look after himself. Perhaps he thought he didn't need the shepherd. Or it could be he didn't like the other sheep.

Sometimes we are like that sheep. We think we don't need anybody. We think we can look after ourselves. So we wander off to find nicer things to do instead of going to church and being with our friends. We go to a beach on a nice warm sunny Sunday. Of course, there is nothing wrong with going to the beach and having a lovely swim. Or we might be invited to a birthday party on a Sunday. There is nothing wrong with birthday parties either.

Is it wrong for the sheep to eat other grass? No, I do not think so. The problem is he did not keep his eyes on the Good Shepherd and the sheep. He got lost.

The good news is, the Good Shepherd missed the lost sheep and he did not say, "Well I still have nine other sheep, it does not matter if one is lost."

No, the Good Shepherd went out to look for the lost sheep because he loved him just as much as the other nine sheep. He didn't want him to be lost so he kept looking for him until he found him and brought him safely back to the others.

Jesus is our Good Shepherd. He does not want us to be lost. He chose to come and bring us back to him. What a great shepherd we have.

The Good Samaritan

One day Jesus told the people who followed him they should first of all love God with all their hearts and then love their neighbours as they loved themselves. Someone in the crowd called out, "But who is my neighbour?"

Perhaps he lived on a farm and did not have any neighbours. Or maybe he lived in a big building with lots of units and had many people around him. Or did he think he was smart and was challenging Jesus?

Jesus said to him, "A man walked in the street and was beaten and robbed."

We hear these things happening every day, don't we? I suppose they took his money, perhaps his mobile phone or iPod and watch. They left him on the road very badly injured. He could not move.

A priest came along. He saw the man lying there but he was on his way to a meeting all dressed up. He thought, "I have no time to help the poor man, I am sure someone else will come soon and will attend to him." So he left him there for someone else to help him.

Next came another man, a Jew (the same nationality as the man who was robbed). He looked and thought, "I don't know what to do. Someone else will know what to do. I'll leave it to someone else." So he crossed to the other side of the road.

Then along came a Samaritan. The Jews did not like the Samaritans and the Samaritans did not like the Jews. This man thought, "I don't like the Jew and he doesn't like me. He wouldn't like me to touch him but he needs help. I am going to help him, never mind if I like him or not." So he took him to a motel and gave the motel owner some money and asked him to look after him. He said when he came back he would drop in and see if he was still there and if more money was needed, he would pay for it.

Now Jesus asked, "Who was the good neighbour to the man who was robbed?"

Who do **you** think was the good neighbour?

What would you do if you saw someone hurt who you didn't like?

What do you think Jesus would have done?

Prayer: Dear Lord, help me to be good, kind and helpful to anyone who needs my help, even if I do not like that person. Amen.

Ten People Healed of Leprosy

Leprosy is a very nasty skin disease and is contagious. That is a big word. If you get close to that person, you could catch leprosy also. So people with leprosy are not allowed to come close to you or anyone else.

Ten men were sick and were not allowed to go home. They were not allowed to go shopping. They were not allowed to go anywhere where healthy people were. I think they became mates and looked after each other, don't you?

One day, they found out that Jesus was going through the town but they were not allowed into town. There was a big hill and they could look down and see Jesus from a distance. They wanted to see Jesus because they heard Jesus could heal them. They would love to talk to him but how could they?

When they saw Jesus coming out with a lot of people around him, they yelled at the top of their voices, "Jesus, please feel sorry for us."

Jesus did hear them and looked up to them and said, "Alright, go to the priest to show that you are healed."

Off they went and soon found out that they were healed. How happy they were. Now they could go back to their families.

But one of them said, "I want to go back to thank Jesus for what he has done for me."

The other nine did not go back with him. I wonder why not? Perhaps they were so keen to go back to their families. Or perhaps they did not care who healed them, they were healed and that was all they wanted.

All ten should have gone back to say "thank you" don't you think?

Don't forget to say "thank you" if your prayers are answered, will you? We often ask God for something and if we get it, we forget to say thank you.

Remember to say "thank you" to Jesus.

The Lord's Prayer

The Lord's Prayer starts with "Our Father in Heaven".

Do you know that you have a father in heaven? Two fathers. One father here where we live and one in Heaven. How exciting.

Some of you might not even have a father here, which is very sad, of course. Perhaps he lives far away and you don't see him very often. But our Father in heaven is always here with us... and you know what? When we want to talk to him, he is never too tired to listen to us... even when you talk to him in the middle of the night.

Just because we cannot see him or touch him, does not mean he is not there. Jesus tells us that he loves us and wants to take care of us. Jesus tells us all about God the Father in the Bible. He says that God the Heavenly Father is full of love. God loves us very much. He even sent his only son to this earth to tell us all about him. God the Father even let Jesus die on the cross for us.

Isn't it great to know that we have such a wonderful Heavenly Father that we can talk to? We can tell him about everything that is bothering us.

I am so glad that we have a Heavenly Father and can always talk to him, aren't you?

Talk to him before you go to bed and tell him all about yourself. Ask him to bless your mum and dad and, of course, your brothers and sisters.

Not only is he your Father but he is also OUR Father. He is my Father also. If we have the same Heavenly Father, then we are family. Isn't it great to know that we are one big family so that we can love and take care of each other?

Prayer:
Thank you, Lord, for loving me. Thank you that I can always talk to you and that you always have time to listen. Amen.

Jesus said, "I will always be with you."

"I will be with you always." Jesus promised this to his friends.

Can we trust Jesus to keep his promises? Yes I believe with all my heart we can trust Jesus.

What about us? Do we keep our promises?

When Mum asks you to clean your bedroom and you are watching your favourite TV show, it is easy to say, "I promise I will do it after the program."

But when the show is finished, you watch something else, or do something else. In no time at all, it is bedtime and Mum will say, "You promised to clean your bedroom and you have not done it."

You might say, "I promise, Mum, I will do it tomorrow."

You do not do it the next day either and Mum starts to nag you about it.

We don't always keep our promises, do we? But we should. If we don't, other people will not trust us anymore.

It is very important to be trusted, and I am so glad we can trust Jesus to keep his promises. If we are his friends and want to follow him, we can fully trust him and know that he will never leave us or forsake us. I am so glad Jesus is my friend.

Is he your friend too?

A Sad Day

One day you may have been very nice and helpful. Mum was so pleased she said: "Let us go and buy you a nice ice cream."

We like to be rewarded for being good, don't we?

The Lord Jesus lived on earth many years ago and he did many good things, too many to count. He healed the sick. He told us to love God and each other. He told us to forgive each other. He told us how much God loves us. He was good every day and never did anything wrong. He showed us the way to God, but some people did not like that and wanted to get rid of him. They had him killed. That is not a reward for being good is it?

We call the day that Jesus died **"Good Friday,"** but it was not a good day for Jesus. Why do we call it good? The Bible tells us, that we all are sinners and are not ready for heaven. Something had to be done. Jesus was willing to come and die for us, so that we can go to heaven. He promised if we believe in him, we will be in heaven with him one day.

We got the reward because of what he did for us. Now we can go to heaven. It became a good day for us.

Thank you, Lord Jesus, for loving us so much.

Jesus Is Alive

One day a lady by the name of Mary Magdalene had been very sick, then she met Jesus and He made her better. How happy she was. She was so happy and loved Jesus so much so that she wanted to be near him all the time and serve him. I think she might have done some cooking and washing for him, don't you?

But something horrible happened to Jesus. Some men killed him and now he was gone. Jesus was put in a tomb and a very big stone was put in front of the tomb.

On Sunday morning, Mary and some other ladies went to the tomb and they noticed that the big stone had been removed. Who could have done that? The other ladies wanted to go back home quickly so that they could tell all Jesus' friends about this. But Mary Magdalene would not leave the tomb and kept on crying and thought that someone had taken Jesus away.

Suddenly she heard a man say, "Why are you crying?"

She thought that this man was a gardener and perhaps had removed Jesus' body. So she said, "Please, sir, tell me where you have taken him."

"Mary" the voice said, and then she recognized Jesus' voice. Oh, how happy she was to hear his voice and know he was alive. How amazing. God brought Jesus back to life again. Yes, Jesus is alive... Mary Magdalene had to tell all his friends that he was alive and that he wanted to see them. I am sure she was happy to tell this good news to everyone.

Paul the Missionary

What is a missionary? It is someone who is on a mission. He or she has a special job to do. Paul had a job to do for God. He did not believe that Jesus was God's Son and his job was to get rid of those who did and put them in jail. He went from town to town to arrest them. One day he and some of his mates went to a city named Damascus. They knew there were some followers of Jesus living there and he was going to bring them back to Jerusalem to have them put into jail.

He was nearly in Damascus when suddenly he saw a very bright light. The light blinded him. He could not see anymore but he heard a voice saying, "Paul, why are you hurting me?"

Paul asked (he couldn't see anything), "Who are you, Lord?"

"I am Jesus," was the answer.

Then Jesus told him to go to Damascus and visit a man named Ananias. Ananias would tell him what to do. Paul's friends led him to the place where Ananias lived because Paul was blind.

When Ananias was told that Paul was on his way to his place, he was frightened. He knew what Paul was up to. But the Lord told him not to worry because he had great plans for Paul.

When Paul arrived at his home, Ananias prayed for him and Paul's eyes were opened and he could see all the beautiful trees and flowers again. Paul understood now that Jesus was the Son of God. His spiritual eyes were opened and he was very sorry for what he had done to the friends of Jesus.

God knew that Paul's heart was right but that he had been on the wrong track. From that day onwards, Paul became a missionary for Jesus. He became the greatest missionary. He travelled all around the world to tell everyone that Jesus is God's Son and that Jesus loves them very much.

Would you like to be a missionary for Jesus?